Banty Rooster

The Story of My Life

LEON SMITH

a.k.a BANTY ROOSTER

Introduction

This is my way of getting you interested enough to read the whole story. (Lee Smith is an eighty-five-year-old male born on August 10, 1931.)

It has been an awesome, wonderful eight-five years filled with adventures, good jobs, fun, and learning unbelievable things I want to pass on to you.

I am the oldest of eight children born to a very poor family. We moved from farm to farm, and I had six different homes before I was sixteen years old. I realize that if you ask two people to describe a telephone pole, they will not give the same answers, as they are looking with two different sets of eyes. I am going to ramble about my life as I saw it through my eyes.

I do not cuss, lie, steal, cheat, or exaggerate. I don't have to. I was raised on farms with animals—cows, horses, pigs, chickens, and dogs, of course. They were my best friends and members of my family. I served twenty-five years in the military (US Army) during two wars—the Korean War in 1950 and Vietnam during the Tet Offensive in 1968. Thirty men were killed in action while jungle fighting in Vietnam, and more than one hundred were wounded. I have had small businesses, and I drove an eighteen-wheeler big rig for twenty-five years. I loved my jobs and retired when I was seventy-five years old, rich enough to do anything I want. Am I bragging? Yep. Do I have a huge ego? Yep! I have earned the right to be me: Banty Rooster.

I am writing this book to pass on to you some of the things I have learned that you can use. For example: Have you been stung by a honeybee or bitten by a fire ant? Just touch the affected area with a copper penny, and the pain will be gone immediately—so fast it will scare you. Do you like collard greens? Do you like the smell of collard greens cooking? Drop a whole uncracked pecan in the pot, and there will be no smell. Do you like chocolate? Is it fattening? The calories in chocolate are scared of heights, so if you hold it over your head or store it on top of the refrigerator, the calories will jump out and you can eat all the chocolate you want. If you get chocolate on your fingers, you are eating too slowly.

I will give you many more details on the subjects I have mentioned above later.

Lee Smith

Banty Rooster Disclaimer

This book was designed and written to provide entertainment in the areas covered. It is sold with the understanding that neither the author nor publisher is advocating any philosophy, public policy, or actions.

Nothing in this book should be taken as the opinions or policies of any employer, associate, or contractor associated with the author in the past, present, or future.

Events herein are portrayed purely on the best memory of the author and should be taken as such and used with discretion by any reader. No assertion of complete historical accuracy is made.

Key names have been disguised or changed to protect the innocent. The purpose of this work is to educate and entertain its readers. The author and publisher shall have no liability to any person or entity with respect to any loss or damage suffered directly or indirectly by the information contained in this book.

I think I should start by defining the term *banty rooster*. The correct name is bantam rooster, which has been shortened to banty rooster through normal speaking in the English language. A banty rooster is a small fighting rooster born with a feisty attitude—walking with his chest out, posing, strutting his stuff, and commanding the attention and obedience of others in his vicinity. He is born with this attitude ingrained into his breed.

I was in the US Army in 1952, assigned to Fort Dix, New Jersey, as the first sergeant of a unit, teaching drafted young men to be soldiers. As top sergeant, one of my duties was to inspect the company area and correct any deficiencies I found. I had a reputation of being an aggressive, demanding supervisor. In the old days in the army, if you had enough rank, you could get away with this. As I moved through the unit area, I could hear my men warning other soldiers, "Banty Rooster is coming. Banty Rooster is coming."

I used that handle for years while in the army and on the CB radios when I was driving the eighteen-wheelers. My men named me. It keeps me strutting my stuff. By the way, I never did tell my men I could hear them spreading the word.

Chapter 1

My Younger Years with My Family

I have decided that I will tell the story of my life based on my age at the time of the event. I was born in August 1931—a healthy, warm-blooded American boy. When I was three years old, my mother gave me a bath. While she was gone to get the clothes to dress me, I ran out the door and down the street buck naked, running as fast as I could go. Soon, my mother and grandmother were chasing me down. My mother loved telling that story to everyone she met.

My father had very little education (about third-grade level), resulting in our family living on farms so he could feed his family by growing food in gardens; having a cow to provide milk and butter; and making apple butter, jellies, jams, and so forth. We canned vegetables, fruits, and meats in tin cans or mason jars. Plastic had not been invented before these times during the middle 1930s and early 1940s. I was more than seventy years old before cell phones were invented. Take a good look at what you missed!

We did not have electricity, radios, televisions, or home-delivered newspapers and were mostly out of contact with the outside world. When I was seven years old, our home sat in the middle of a large open field with no neighbors within four hundred yards. We had two cherry trees, a hand-operated pump to pull the water out of the ground, and a very large garden for growing beans, lettuce, potatoes, sweet potatoes, sweet corn, and the like. Mostly, all we needed from the stores were flour, cornmeal, sugar, coffee, shoes, and clothes for the kids. Daddy made approximately fifty dollars per month, and we got by on that.

In the summer, a group of us kids would walk about three miles to a movie theater to watch a picture show. I remember if we walked on a blacktop road, it would be so hot our feet would end up burned. The tickets to the theater were eleven cents each, if I remember correctly. Just before the movie started, there would be about ten minutes of news about the outside world. When I was ten years old, I was walking to school and saw in the window of a small grocery store the headline of a newspaper with the words "The United States Declares War on Japan." That's how we learned about Pearl Harbor on December 7, 1941.

Chapter 2

When I Was Ten Years Old: Pearl Harbor and World War II

In 1941 Japan was ruled by an emperor who also had a warlord. Japan needed oil and space for its population. This warlord wanted to attack the United States on its western shores. When he was advised that every American home had weapons to be used for hobbies and hunting, this warlord changed his mind and decided to attack the US Navy in Pearl Harbor. This began the war in the South Pacific, which was part of World War II—thanks to the Second Amendment of our Constitution.

And we were also a member of the Allies fighting against Germany in Europe (known as the Nazis). This was a very critical time in our history—fighting against two enemies dedicated to taking over our United States of America, wanting us to speak German and Japanese. After Pearl Harbor, a Japanese official stated, "We have woken up a sleeping giant." This happened to be true.

Fathers left their jobs and joined the military to fight our enemies until they were destroyed. Farmers stayed behind to grow foods that were sorely needed by both civilians to raise kids and soldiers to win wars.

Mothers took their own children to other people's homes where three or four mothers would take care of ten to fourteen children. These children's own mothers went away from home to work in defense plants making ammunition, airplanes, and submarines—anything to help fight the Germans and Japanese. The next time you see an elderly lady, just remember what she and her parents went through to give you this free country you have today.

This was December 1941. After the Pearl Harbor attack, our government gathered up all the Japanese in the United States and put them in camps to prevent them from sabotaging our defense plants or anything that would help the Japanese government. We were at war with Japan.

In those days, many Americans were called rednecks. These were strong-minded males who may have gone to a bar and after a few beers it would be just like them to go hunting for "slant-eyes." This would not be good for the Japanese people. Putting the Japanese in these camps protected them from harm. We took them from their homes, businesses, and the freedom the United States had provided for them. They owned farms, grew food, and were living the American dream. They were in these camps until the end of the war. The American government paid them millions of dollars, trying to repay them for what they had lost.

I was a teenager during all of this. We never looked back. We just took everything in stride along with everyone else. It was the only way we knew, and it made a bunch of good Americans—now known as the Greatest Generation.

During the Korean War and the Vietnam War, our American soldiers spent twelve to thirteen months in the war zone. During World War II, our soldiers and mothers were signed up for the duration of the war. As Gen. Dwight Eisenhower put it on June 2, 1944, before the landing on D-day: "We will accept nothing less than full Victory!"

Our Americans and our Allies put everything on the line to ensure that we would win World War II. They, we, did!

Our president at that time made the decision to drop a couple of atomic bombs on Japan, resulting in killing close to one million Japanese people in their own country. This also saved thousands of American soldiers who would have died trying to drive the Japanese out of the islands in the Pacific Ocean. The Japanese had dug tunnels and put up defenses that would have taken months, or even years, to dig out. After the atomic bombs, the Japanese surrendered. Americans gave a sigh of relief and went about living the American way. Our mothers and fathers came home, had a major celebration, and went back to work.

Chapter 3

My Teenage Years and Starting to Grow Up

My family had moved to another farm with the normal animals. At twelve years of age, my brother and I would cut wood with an ax and a crosscut saw that we could use to take care of all the cooking and heating needs of our house. We did this after school and on weekends. We also worked for some neighbors who had thirty-five dairy cows that had to be milked by hand twice daily. My pay in those days was fifteen cents per hour.

When I was sixteen years old, I had a twenty-six-year-old uncle who moved in with our family and worked on the farms for twenty cents an hour. After a couple of weeks working on the farm, the owner raised his pay to twenty-five cents per hour and mine to twenty cents an hour, saying I was not old enough to need twenty-five cents an hour.

I told the owner that I was not going to work for twenty cents an hour till I was twenty-five years old. I was learning to rule my life, so I quit working for him.

He gave me a raise, and I quit. My uncle and I bought a 1931 Dodge sedan with wooden spokes in the wheels and a tar paper top. We paid one hundred dollars (fifty dollars each). This gave us transportation to seek better jobs. About three weeks later, I paid my uncle fifty dollars for his share in the Dodge, and he moved out of our home.

When I was seventeen years old, I left home and moved into an uncle's house twelve miles away from my parents' home. That was far away from my family—a long ways. I got a job paying forty-five cents per hour, forty hours per week. I had learned to not accept less. I have always lived my life seeking more.

Understand that in those days, there were not many automobiles on the roads. Having a car had a great deal to do with my learning to grow up. That takes a long time.

Chapter 4

Growing Up and Leaving Home, 1948

When I was seventeen years old, a buddy of mine and I went to the West Virginia coal mines to get a job. Being country boys used to seeing green grass and blue sky, mining coal was not for us. After looking and searching, we decided that we did not want to go into a hole in the ground with a light on our hats so could see. In order to see what these coal mines were like we needed to drive down deep, dirt, mountain roads—very steep and very deep roads. Big trucks loaded with six tons of coal would only go six or seven miles per hour up those steep roads. When we decided we did not want to be miners and had to go back up those steep roads, my '31 Dodge did not want to climb up the steep hills. We determined that there was a hole in the diaphragm of the fuel pump so it could not feed enough gas to run the motor up hills that steep. *Well* ... reverse gear would put the gas tank higher than the motor, thus gravitating the gasoline into the motor. Weren't we smart!

We decided to climb up those steep hills in reverse gear. That worked like a charm—of course, it takes a long time to back up six or seven miles in reverse gear, but it was worth it. We went back home in Virginia.

Chapter 5

Joining the Army and Going to Japan

At seventeen years old, I joined the National Guard. At eighteen years old, I joined the US Army on November 7, 1948. I finished basic training and was sent to Japan in the spring of 1949. That's when life got a lot more exciting. This was four years after the end of the Japanese and American war. Occupation duty in Japan was soldiers' paradise.

The average Japanese policeman guarding our compound made approximately $10.00 per month. As a private in the army, my pay was about $50.00 per month. We paid a Japanese man $4.50 a month to clean our barracks, shine our shoes, and take care of our needs. With the money he was making working for the US Army, he was a big wheel in the village just outside of the compound where we lived. My duty hours were from six o'clock in the morning until five o'clock in the evening. My job was defending the commanding general in a time of peace. The requirement to be a member of this platoon of thirty men was to be able to down a half a pint of whiskey in one drink. I was eighteen years old and dumb in April 1950.

On June 25, 1950, North Korea surprised attacked South Korea, and the Korean War started. There were few American troops in South Korea, and they immediately went on defense trying to stop the North Koreans from conquering South Korea. My outfit immediately began training for war, exercising, practicing defense methods, and so on. All of this was in Japan.

Chapter 6

Communism and the Korean War—Invasion at Inchon

My understanding is that communism (socialism) is a situation where the government controls everything you do. It would tell you what career you would work, when to go to work, and when to stop work. It would tell you where you live and how you act. If you were a farmer and grew one thousand pounds of potatoes, the government would take all of your potatoes. Then they would check your family, determine how many potatoes you need, and give that many back to you.

North Korea was communist, backed by China and Russia. Attacking South Korea was for the purpose of spreading communism. If they could capture South Korea, their intentions were to spread communism to the Philippines, Australia, and eventually North America, including the United States and *you*.

To stop the spread of communism, Gen. Douglas MacArthur had the idea of landing in Korea behind the North Koreans, thus cutting off supplies and communication. This would give us a great advantage. On the first day of September, much of the Seventh Infantry Division was loaded aboard transport ships and left Japan to go hide out in the Pacific Ocean. We stayed out in the ocean for fifteen days.

The ships for the Seventh Infantry Division were supply ships left over from World War II. After World War II, these ships had been anchored in the ocean for five years. They were repaired and upgraded to carry an infantry unit (more than seven thousand armed soldiers), including trucks, tanks, and everything it took to support them.

On approximately September 15, 1950, our convoy of ships began moving into a huge storm. The wind and the water tossed our ship around like a tennis ball in a washing machine. Just after daylight, I came out on deck and was told that a Russian MiG (Russian fighter plane) had just passed over the ship and dropped two bombs that missed our ship.

We threw rope ladders over the side of the ship to a medium-sized landing craft. When we climbed down the ladders, the landing craft took us to the levee where we stepped onto the port of Inchon, Korea. The tides in Inchon are thirty-two feet two times a day. An hour after we got on the levee, we looked back at our landing craft. It was stuck in the mud. They had to wait several hours for the tide to come back in and lift them up so they could go pick up more people to help us to recapture the capital of South Korea. The Seventh Infantry Division and the First Marine division recaptured Seoul, South Korea, the second day in Korea. I think it was the second day. It took door-to-door fighting to capture the city.

For several days, we sat around our foxholes pulling guard duty twenty-four hours a day. Around my foxhole were red peppers. Not caring for hot food, I did not bother the red peppers for a couple of days. Then I nonchalantly reached over, picked one up, and bit into it. My mouth was on fire. These peppers are put in kimchi, a very common Korean food. *Woo-wee! It was hot!* I never bit into red peppers again. A couple of days later we climbed aboard trucks and convoyed toward Pusan, South Korea. After fifteen to twenty miles, we were ambushed by North Koreans. I remember lying in a ditch and firing into some trees. It was not long before the ambushers ran away. We climbed back on the trucks and continued the convoy to Pusan.

Chapter 7
More Korean War—the Invasion of North Korea

When we got to Pusan, we were put to pulling guard duty outside of the war room. I peeked through a crack in the canvas where I could see maps showing American positions in Korea. At about eleven o'clock one night, one of our guards caught a man inside of our perimeter peeking into a crack in the tent of the war room. The guard opened fire, and the spy climbed a fence post with a barbed wire on it. The spy got away. Come morning, we found blood on the fence post.

Several days later we were loaded aboard ships and set out to sail north off the east coast of Korea. Three of us were put on a submarine. That night at about ten o'clock we were taken off the submarine and put on a small landing craft. This was at Iwon Beach, North Korea. It was November 8, 1950.

We were given instructions to patrol north and south at least one mile up and down the beach and inland to look for the enemy. We did this in two to three hours. Nobody fired at us, so we shined a flashlight out to sea, and the landing craft came back, picked us up, and took us back to the submarine.

The next morning, a couple of hours after daylight, the submarine surfaced, and we went up on deck. Wow … there were minesweepers searching for mines in the same part of the ocean that had nothing on it last night except us three snoopers. There were ships, boats, trucks on the beach, and several thousand soldiers unloading on the beach with equipment of all kinds. I remember two things the most: First, there were men stringing communication wire all over the sandy beach in every direction while trucks, jeeps, and soldiers were getting off the landing craft. This completely ruined all the wire everybody was putting out. Lordy, Lordy. Second, a young soldier was driving a jeep and smoking a cigarette. I saw a general wave the jeep to a stop and proceeded to chew that young soldier out for smoking a cigarette while driving a jeep. I was five steps from them. A couple thousand soldiers fighting a war, and this. Lordy, Lordy.

This was about November 9, 1950. The next twenty days were spent moving from the Iwon Beach to the Yalu River—sometimes marching, sometimes by truck, but mostly by climbing mountains. We climbed so many mountains that I had calluses on the front of my ankles. If I remember correctly, we had the old-type boots with the two buckles on them. Not encountering the enemy very much, we ended up running the North Korean Army out of North Korea … The Yalu River separates China from North Korea.

Chapter 8

The Chinese Army Joined the War

The computer says that on November 28, I was patrolling west on the Yalu River with the Seventeenth Regimental Combat Team. I remember the night when I was standing up looking down on the Yalu River. It was frozen—ice covered with virgin snow. There was not a mark on that snow when I crawled into my foxhole. The next morning when I got up, it looked like ten thousand mice had been running back and forth across the river. It was the Chinese ... the Chinese Army.

We grabbed our equipment and started marching south. I know that we marched about eight hours or eight miles—I don't remember which. It was November 29—no leaves on the trees and snow on the ground. We were in the valley, and looking back at the mountain ridges, we could see the Chinese Army walking down the ridges behind us on the right and left. We came to a convoy parked in the middle of the road. We climbed on to the trucks, drove off, and left the Chinese.

Your computer will tell you that the temperature was thirty-two degrees below zero. I remember that well.

We drove south over the mountains on snow-covered roads and lost equipment due to trucks sliding off the roads. We couldn't take time to save the equipment. The Chinese were coming. We went past the Chosen Reservoir, North Korea. (Look that one up your computer: Chosen Reservoir, North Korea, December 1950.) We were headed for Hamhung and Hungnam, North Korea.

When we got there, five of us were placed on top of a three-story school building with a .50-caliber machine gun. Our job was to sit there with one man behind the machine gun with his finger on the trigger, looking for Russian MiG fighter planes. If a MiG showed up, coming out of the skyline, we would probably only have about five seconds to shoot at him, so we had to have a finger on the trigger.

By the way, somehow I had jammed my middle finger on my right hand, and it was swollen twice as big as normal. I was using heat tablets (used to heat food rations) to heat water in a canteen cup to soak my swollen finger. I don't remember that helping much.

Chapter 9

Defending from Chinese and Saving Korean Citizens

This was about December 20, 1950. From where we sat, we could watch our jet airplanes dropping napalm gas on targets far off in front of us. Napalm gas is a jellylike gas. When the jet airplanes were flying low, speeding over the ground, and dropping napalm bombs at a high rate of speed, the jelly gas would splash several hundred yards. This gas would stick to everything and burn everything, putting off lots of heat that destroyed the enemy and their equipment. Thank you to the US Air Force.

Like I said, we could see this burning napalm gas splashing on the ground 180 degrees from my right to my left. This was on December 23, 1950.

The Korean civilian population had been coming for days from the north to the south, running from the Chinese. There would be groups of people, five to eight Koreans wide, leading hundreds of yards of people behind them carry everything they owned on their heads and backs—running from the Chinese communists. These Korean mothers, fathers, grandparents, and children had no expressions on their faces—no anger, no passion, no nothing. Just dead expressions. These lost Koreans would end up on the beaches.

On December 23, the beaches were full of these Koreans. They were being loaded on large landing craft that would hold seventy or more people. That afternoon those LSTs (landing ship, tanks) left the beaches and sailed out of sight, taking the Koreans to where I do not know.

By December 23, our planes were dropping napalm 180 degrees from the coast on our left to the coast on my right. The word was that the Chinese had so many soldiers that when you shot one with a rifle, there were more than four others to pick up his rifle and continue to fight.

The USS *Missouri* was sitting behind us in the ocean so far we could not see it. When the *Missouri* fired off those thirty-inch cannons, they lit up the whole countryside. The loud *boom* sound of the shots came after the rounds from the cannons had passed overhead. That made quite a picture. Down on the beaches they were piling our equipment—our American equipment—in twenty- or thirty-foot piles with fifty-gallon tanks of gasoline in the piles. The idea was that we would shoot into the barrels, start fires, and burn up all equipment so the Chinese would not be able use it. We had no way to take that piled-up equipment off the beaches, and they were putting as many Korean citizens as they could on LST landing crafts. We watched as these LSTs sailed away out of sight on the evening of December 23, 1950.

Chapter 10

Leaving North Korea for South Korea, Christmas 1950

Midmorning on December 24, Christmas Eve, our group with our machine gun was loaded on a ship and sent below deck. I was informed that enemy mortar rounds were hitting the water as we sailed away from the beach. At about midnight, December 24, 1950 we got off the ship in Pusan, South Korea. There was no Red Cross with coffee and doughnuts waiting for us.

We boarded a Korean train and were given five-in-one rations to eat (one meal for five people). The train carried us all that night and most of the next day (Christmas Day). We got off the train about two hours before dark on Christmas Day. Blue Ribbon Brewery had donated beer (one can each) to the soldiers for Christmas plus paper and envelopes so we could write home. They gave us Christmas presents, toothbrushes, toothpaste, chocolate bars, and Life-Savers candies.

I had been assigned a guard position, so I put on my two-tone poncho. It was white on one side and green on the other side—green for summer and white for snow. I put the white on the outside because it was snowing big, beautiful, white snowflakes with no wind. Large snowflakes gently fell to the ground, not freezing. Just think about it: A full belly of hot food and a clear night with a big moon showing off the snowflakes falling gently to the ground. One of our tanks was parked a short distance away with a radio softly playing country music. It was a beautiful night—Christmas night, a night to remember. I had not heard any music since September.

Chapter 11

Moving North in South Korea

For the next couple of weeks, things were pretty quiet. I remember moving through a mountain pass that was quickly closed by the Chinese. We could not go back through the pass for a couple of weeks. Consequently, flying boxcars would fly over us and drop parachutes with water, ammunition, and corned beef hash. We did not need the ammunition, because we were not fighting. We did not need the water, because there was snow on the ground. After a couple of days, who needed corned beef hash? Still, we got ammunition, water, and corned beef hash.

Two of us watched deer pass between our foxholes one night. We decided to get some deer meat. The next day we followed the deer tracks. When we came to some brush around a couple of trees, two deer jumped out of the bushes and started running. We got them and cooked them with potatoes that we dug out of the holes in the ground. It was quite an improvement over corned beef hash.

At some point during this time, I inherited a 57 mm recoilless rifle team. The following is how I remembered it sixty-six years ago.

A recoilless rifle is about four feet long, weighs about fifty pounds, and has a barrel about three feet long. The barrel was about as big around as a tennis ball. The chamber where you load the weapon is five times larger than the barrel. The brass that holds the powder that fires the weapon is perforated with about a hundred holes. When the weapon is fired, a projectile goes out the barrel of the weapon and can be accurate to a target 1,200 yards away. This projectile can be HE (high explosive) or HEAT (high explosive antitank). It's a nice weapon to have around when you need it.

The team consisted of a gunner, assistant gunner, and two men to carry four rounds each. The gunner aims and fires the weapon, the assistant gunner loads the weapon and then looks to the rear of the weapon to ensure it is clear before he taps the gunner on top of the head to tell him it's ready. When the weapon is fired, the projectile goes out of the front of the weapon, and a blast of hot, exploded gas, two thousand to three thousand degrees, goes out of the rear of the weapon. *You don't want any of your people to get hurt.*

Before you fire this weapon, you pick which direction you're going run. As soon as you fire, every enemy within range is going to shoot into your area. Say bye-bye fast and seek cover.

Chapter 12

Using a 57 mm Recoilless Rifle

On a warm April day in early afternoon, I was looking across a valley when I saw three of our tanks coming up the middle of the valley on a dirt road. The next thing I saw was three enemy soldiers crossing a field toward the creek that was running between the field and the tanks. The enemy was carrying what appeared to be a three-and-a-half-inch rocket launcher, which is an antitank weapon.

I immediately got on my radio and tried to raise my company commander. He, in turn, could relay the information to the battalion commander, who could warn the tanks about the antitank weapon at about four o'clock on their right rear. Even though I could not raise anybody, I relayed that message on my radio for all who could hear it. I stated I would fire my 57 mm recoilless rifle with a white phosphorus round (gives off white smoke), noting a position on the terrain. I fired that round in the creek about fifty yards from where the enemy went into the creek. A short time later, the tanks were coming up on a bridge. The tanks got off the road and turned toward my white phosphorus smoke and fired several rounds into the creek. After that, I don't know what happened. The three-and-a-half-inch rocket launcher never did fire. The tanks turned around and went back to the way they had come. I never found out what happened to the enemy.

A few days later on a warm, sunshiny afternoon we were climbing a mountain, and I noticed that the young men around me were using a lot of profanity. Well, my daddy taught me not to cuss. Shortly after that, an enemy machine gun started firing higher up the mountain. Things got really quiet, and I looked around. All of those young men who had been using profanity had reached into their pockets and were now reading the New Testament. Well, well, well …

One thing I haven't mentioned: In South Korea or at least the northern part of South Korea, there were ditches around the top of every mountain and all the ridges coming off the mountains. The ditches were more than four feet deep. These ditches appeared to have been dug by human hands. I have always wondered how these ditches came to be. There were hundreds of miles of these ditches. Or maybe I should say there was one long, long ditch running for miles and miles.

Chapter 13

Contacted the NVA and R&R

Sometime around April or May 1950 we were in foxholes guarding a hill. Another outfit came and took over our positions in the foxholes, and we moved to the back side of the hill to sleep. The following morning we started moving out toward the North Korean lines to make contact with the North Koreans. We were crossing no-man's-land.

When we got close to the North Korean lines, they fired at us. No one was hurt! We had made contact. We immediately turned around and went back the way we came. When we came to our original foxholes, we passed through them and walked down the mountain.

We had been living on top of the hill where there was no water, and there was no water in no-man's-land, so when we crossed the line of foxholes, we were starving for water. I was still caring the 57 mm recoilless rifle.

My company commander and I were the first to get downhill off the mountain and found a stream to get water. That time, the water tasted good.

Shortly after that, I went on five days R&R in Japan. R&R means rest and relaxation. Early one morning someone yelled,

"Smith, R&R!" I picked up my gear, walked off that hill, and went to an indicated area. Soon, an airplane landed to pick up me and twenty other soldiers. They then carried us to Japan. After landing, we went into a building where they took our weapons, ammo, and gear.

They then gave us anything we wanted to eat. A lot of us ordered hamburgers and french fries. From there, we went to the showers and then to a counter where they gave us khaki uniforms with brass, medals, and a month's pay (cash) to anyone who wanted it. Later, they put us on buses, drove us to downtown Tokyo, and turned us loose for five days. This was approximately seven hours after we'd left our foxholes. For five days we roamed Tokyo doing anything we wanted to, which was eating, drinking, and partying.

Five days later we reported in to the place where we were loaded on the buses that took us to Tokyo. Six hours later we were back with our unit in Korea. We had our gear and M1 rifles with ammunition. Things were quiet after that. Around August 1, 1951, I was sent to Japan. A couple of days later I boarded a ship going to San Francisco.

I crossed under the Golden Gate Bridge on August 10, 1951. That was my twentieth birthday. I had almost a year of combat under my belt.

Chapter 14

Coming Home from Korea, 1951

Before I left Korea, I had received a letter from my girlfriend stating that she had announced our engagement in the newspaper. She included a copy of the announcement. Being young, that was okay with me.

I boarded a passenger train and traveled to Kansas City, Missouri, and stayed there for a couple of days. Then I went on to Roanoke, Virginia, where I got off my bus in the middle of the day. The bus that would take me the forty-five miles to my hometown would not leave until ten o'clock that night.

While messing around in Roanoke, Virginia, I met a young soldier with two girlfriends. With four hours to kill, we went to a movie. After the movie was over, they took me to the bus station. It was close to ten o'clock at night, which was well after dark. As I started to get on the bus, one of the girlfriends gave me a big kiss on the lips and a big hug. After the war I had been in, I was getting civilized!

As we traveled forty-five miles to my hometown, I was talking to all the other passengers. Naturally, I was elated to be coming home. When we pulled up to the bus station, one of the ladies asked me if anybody would be meeting me at the station. I told her I did not think so. That's when she told me that maybe I would want to take the lipstick off my lips and face. I wiped my face with a tissue and found a whole bunch of red lipstick. Thank you, nice lady!

I found a taxi that took me home where no one was awake. I remember that at two thirty in the morning, the taxi driver was telling me how hard he worked and how tough things were. I had nothing to say. No problem. I went to sleep. At six o'clock the next morning, everyone woke me up and welcomed me home. I got lots and lots of hugs! Welcome home!

Understand that in those days, none of my family had telephones, and cell phones had not been invented. My family knew nothing about where I was or when I would be coming home.

About ten days later my girlfriend and I got married. After a seven-day honeymoon, we came back home. I had two dollars left in my pocket, so I got a job helping my father dig a foundation for a large church. I worked on that for about ten days at three dollars per hour for ten-hour days. Three hundred dollars was a lot of money.

A few days later I picked up my duffel bag full of my army uniforms and started hitchhiking to my new assignment. That was 360 miles south to Fort Jackson, South Carolina. I joined an infantry unit whose mission was to make newly sworn in civilians into soldiers.

Chapter 15
Leadership School, Good Training

I was sent to a four-week leadership school where I was taught how to teach classes, method of instruction, and so forth. It was stressed that if the students fail to learn, the teacher failed to teach, which made sense to me.

Leadership school taught me a lot about how to be a leader of men. The following is a list of things to guide any supervisor:

1. The five Ps: prior planning prevents poor performance.
2. Inspect, detect, and correct. (You don't know what's going on till you look. Then take action.)
3. Delegate. If you do the work, five don't. If you don't work, five do. Supervising gets the job done correctly, quickly, and to the proper standards.
4. Discipline. You break the rules, you pay. It's important to do what's needed without supervision.
5. Promptness. Be on time.
6. Get involved, stay involved. Experience counts; you learn.
7. Be honest, because you will get caught.

The above are rules to live by. Made up by me.

Chapter 16

Teaching Army Basic Training and Becoming a Drill Sergeant

Let's set up the situation. I am a member of a military organization that takes young men who woke up in their mothers' houses yesterday morning. They reported to a designated area, and today were loaded on buses and brought to my company in civilian clothes. My company consists of a number of experienced soldiers (called cadre) who are to turn these young men into fighting soldiers in fourteen to sixteen weeks. At the end of this basic training, these young men will most surely be sent to fight the Korean War. We will receive between 200 and 250 of these young men on this day. When these loaded buses arrive in our unit, a group of experienced soldiers start yelling for them to get off those buses at double-time speed.

These experienced soldiers are now known as drill sergeants. You may forget your father's name, but you will never forget your first drill sergeant's name.

Chapter 17

Introducing New Troops to the Army

We have these new arrivals put down everything they carry. Next, we run them to the barbershop where they get a haircut—a close, GI haircut. We then take them to a warehouse where they are issued uniforms, shoes, socks, towels, underwear, hats, and caps. We ensure that all of this clothing fits their body to military standards.

We will receive 200 to 250 men that day. After they are done with the arrival procedures, we will take them to the barracks where they will live for the next four months. Welcome home!

The rest of the day will be used to feed them supper and indoctrinate them on the rules and standards needed to live with their new family. Lessons will include: taking showers, cleaning their sleeping areas, shining their boots, and conducting themselves properly toward each other, including no stealing from the family. At ten o'clock at night, it's lights out and time to be in bed. These men's lives have been totally changed today. We will see them again the next morning at five o'clock. That's quite a day!

The next sixteen weeks will be used to make them physically fit, disciplined, and mentally prepared to go to war. They will have learned marksmanship, familiarity with rifles and machine guns, and how to administer first aid to their fellow wounded men (stop the bleeding, protect the wound, and prevent shock). Later, they may get jobs not connected to the infantry; however, they may always be called on to perform as infantrymen when the situation requires it.

In January 1951, many of those young men were sent to the Korean War, and the cadre of my unit received another 200 to 250 men to put through the paces again. I trained young soldiers for about twelve years during my career—approximately nine thousand men whom I could call by name at one time or another. I am also proud of that!

Chapter 18

Transferred to Hawaii, the Cuban Crisis

I stated that I was going to ramble about the story of my life. That's what I'm doing. I taught sergeants to be drill sergeants in 1956 and 1957. Then, in 1958, my family and I were transferred to Hawaii. And my family loved it. We stayed at Waikiki Beach for several weeks until we found housing. My family went to the beach and swam in the ocean on Christmas Eve, which was unheard of back home.

In Hawaii I taught basic trainees and NCO academies. I had a good time teaching American soldiers to not be caught asleep on guard duty. It is not fun for them.

During the Cuban crisis, when the Russians put submarines in Cuba, I was only allowed to be fifteen minutes from a telephone and thirty minutes from my company. If I got a call on one of my contact phone numbers and somebody said, "cocked pistol," I had thirty minutes to start loading my unit on airplanes. We had a couple of dry runs doing that. You improve with practice.

Chapter 19

ROTC at the University of Missouri

In 1961 I applied for and received assignment to the University of Missouri to teach military science to ROTC cadets. This was a three-year tour. I was teaching a class when President John F. Kennedy was assassinated.

I also managed the drill team who provided honor guards to the American flag before Missouri football games. And I was the coach of the Missouri rifle teams. Here I go, bragging again.

The fifty-foot rifle range used to practice marksmanship was located in cement basement of a three-story classroom building. I placed felt padding on the walls and hung it from the ceilings to cushion the crack of rifle fire, making it easier on the ears. The Missouri rifle team was rated eighth out of the Big Ten universities in that area. Eighth out of ten? The only place we could go was up.

I read up on marksmanship. The book said the rear aperture sights should be 60 mm. I checked the rear sights of the rifles we had and found that the sights were 20 mm. The 20 mm setting gave false impressions. Without telling the students (rifle team shooters), I changed all the rear sights on their rifles to 60 mm.

The students who were firing the rifles complained and

complained and complained. And their scores went up and up and up. A year later Missouri was eighth and ninth out of ten. Alaska was hard to beat. We ended up with two All-American shooters that year.

Chapter 20

Campus Conduct and Actions

When I first arrived at the University of Missouri, I was briefed to not get into political confrontations with students. This was in the days of arguments against the administration. I was alerted to the fact that students would ask questions, knowing what my answer would be, and I would be forced to put my foot in my mouth. I was tempted but never got involved in any of this.

One afternoon I left my office after five o'clock. Just after I turned toward my car, a beautiful young lady stepped out from between two cars. As she approached me, she asked me for the time. She had on beautiful, tight-fitting clothes, orange earrings, and orange lipstick. She was dressed to a T—capital *T*. She stated that she was supposed to meet her boyfriend, but he hadn't showed up. Even though she could see it, I told her I didn't have a watch. I got in my car and drove home. I could have made the newspapers.

On college campuses you could find black bras at the top of our flagpoles.

Chapter 21

Teaching Patriotism to Young Americans

On Wednesday afternoons at four o'clock, we had parades with other ROTC groups in full dress uniform. I would be in full dress uniforms with my gold oversea bars, time in service bars, and all the medals and ribbons I had collected in my twelve years, including my eleven months in the Korean War. My job was to walk behind the cadets as they stood at attention.

If someone was too tense, his neck would turn white, indicating he was ready to pass out and fall to the ground. My job was to catch him and ease him to the ground and then look for another white neck. Just behind the cadets were university buildings with steps holding fifteen to twenty-five regular students. The students were laughing and enjoying the afternoon.

When the National Anthem started playing as the flag was being lowered, the students continued to laugh and giggle. This did not sit right with me. The following Wednesday the same thing happened. On my second Wednesday, this really did not sit right with me.

On my third Wednesday, I walked past the cadets to the last set of steps holding about twenty-five students. I stood tall and called out in a commanding voice: "*Excuse me!*"

Everyone went silent.

Lowering my voice a little, I said, "My generation is concerned about the lack of attention and patriotism your generation is showing to the national anthem and the lowering of the flag. I believe that this happens to be a lack of knowledge rather than a lack of patriotism. When the music starts, you face the flag. If you can't see the flag, face the music. Put your right hand over your heart, and stand tall. The only time you can talk is when you are correcting someone who isn't doing the same. Thank you!"

I received a very sincere, "Thank you, Sergeant," from the students.

I got another set of steps that Wednesday and three sets of steps the fourth Wednesday. After that, nobody moved. I knew they had learned patriotism. They felt goose bumps up and down their spines like the rest of us.

Do not be ashamed to *pass it on*! This lets *you* help build duty, honor, and country.

Chapter 22

Living in a College Atmosphere and Raising Children

For the next three years, I lived in the Columbia, Missouri. There were three different colleges in Columbia, Missouri. Their students lived in every available building with rooms to rent. My wife and I, with our three children (ages five, six, and seven), lived in a one-room basement for two months. After that, I had to buy a mobile home, trading the furniture that we had been storing as a down payment. That was just life in the 1960s.

My whole family, including the children, were very active in the community where we lived. We were just outside the city limits in a farming community. We were in the Boy Scouts and Future Farmers of America. This type of locality is a good place to raise children.

In 1964 I was reassigned to Korea. I left my family in Missouri while I was serving in Korea. It is hard for military mothers to raise children without dads. This is the military life.

Chapter 23

Sentry Dogs, Sentry Dog handlers, and Protecting the Public

In Korea I was put in charge of thirty-two sentry guard dogs whose job was to protect nuclear warheads buried in tunnels. They accomplished this by patrolling every other day for twelve hours a night: four hours on, four hours off, four on, four off. This was the work schedule for the dogs and their handlers for at least one entire year.

Each handler could only have one dog. When he was given a dog, it would remain his friend and family for the next year. No handler could touch another dog. These were one-man dogs. If two dogs got together, they would fight to the death. Over the next year, this happened a couple of times. If one dog got a lock on another dog's neck, it would take a metal rod to pry his mouth open.

By the way, when the dogs were not in their kennels, the handlers had to be armed with loaded .45-caliber pistols. If a dog got free and threatened a human—any human—the handler was to run toward the dog, place his pistol against the dog's body, judge that the bullet would not harm any human, and pull the trigger. If a native Korean was to get hurt, it would make worldwide news. This, we did not need.

While serving occupational duties in the Far East, the word was put out that our enemies to the north were placing females with venereal diseases among the US Army.

Chapter 24

Ambassadors of America

When I received new soldiers from the States, I would pull them to the side and introduce them to being ambassadors of the United States. I would tell them how the bartering system worked. If they wanted to buy something—for instance, a full-sized silk kimono—from the local salespeople, they should ask the price. If they were told $18.00, they should divide that in half, divide that answer in half, and offer that amount (in this example, $4.50). After a bit of bartering, they should pay about $7.50. That was in 1964. Sometimes it is nice to have old-timers around.

I told them that by being the new men on the block, they were considered a good catch by the ladies in the village.

I also told them the way to handle their occupational duties and love life. It was normal for the soldiers to find themselves a girlfriend and pay her ten dollars a month. This would pay her food and rent, and at the end of the month, she would have cigarette and beer money left over. It was a comfortable way to live. I told these new men it was the intelligent way for them to pull occupational duty. I insisted that this was the smart way and stressed for them to take their time finding girlfriends. I would explain: "Do not grab the first one you meet. Give yourself seven days to pick your steady girlfriend. It will be worth the wait and reduces your chances of getting VD tenfold."

Sometimes it is nice having old-timers around.

Chapter 25

Returned to the United States and Family

In mid-1965 I received orders to go to Fort Jackson, South Carolina. I went to Columbia, Missouri, picked up my family, and moved back into the house I have owned and rented out since 1956.

In Fort Jackson I taught basic trainees and Drill Sergeant School again. Just before Christmas I received orders for Vietnam. *Here we go again*, I thought. My reporting date was February 1968. This was to be a completely different world.

During the Korean War, we had battle lines that crossed Korea from the west coast to the east coast. North Korea was north of that battle line, and our Allied forces were south of that battle line. We knew what was ours and what was theirs.

During the Vietnam War, we had bases throughout the country. These bases were miles apart, usually called LZs (landing zones). These LZs were usually less than one mile long and one mile wide and sitting somewhere in the middle of the jungle—at least in northern Vietnam where there were mountains and lots of jungle. The enemy could be 360 degrees in any direction.

Chapter 26

Deployed to the First Air Cavalry in Vietnam

I was assigned to the First Air Cav (Cavalry) division. We supposedly had 450 helicopters, mostly Hueys. That means we got to ride instead of walk most of the time. We could get resupplies of food and ammunition quite easily and have the wounded picked up quickly. These choppers—we called them *birds*—were armed with at least two machine guns and boxes of grenades—extra firepower when you needed it. Normally a chopper could carry eight men with their equipment. If you had to cross high mountains where the air was light, it could carry only six men.

A normal combat assault consisted of five Huey helicopters with eight men each—and other birds carrying in the rest of our unit. We would go into the attack with machine guns firing and men hanging onto the rails and shooting into the bushes from the hip. Real cowboys. We attacked like this as many as eight times in one day, but not often.

At this time, February 1968, I was thirty-six years old, and most of my men were eighteen or nineteen years old. An infantry rifle company was supposed to have 160 men in the jungle. This included medics and engineers. I was lucky if I had eighty men. Because of my rank, I took over as first sergeant and as a platoon leader. First sergeant is known as top sergeant, many times nicknamed *Top*. Because of my years in service, teaching leadership, tactics, and experience, I felt completely at home. Top sergeant set the standard of performance, discipline, attitudes, and lifestyle of the unit. Strange but true.

Chapter 27

Living in a Combat Zone

A couple of comments: I don't remember ever having a feeling of fear or seeing fear in my men while in a combat zone. Or even during a firefight. They just kept doing what needed to be done. And I don't remember cries of pain on the battlefield. I really believe that when you are hit and wounded, your body cushions the pain. And I was around this type of action for more than twenty-four months.

I can remember four different times when booby traps wounded thirteen of my men, and I still do not remember any cries of pain. I was wounded three different times by our own weapons. You have to be wounded by your enemy to receive a Purple Heart. I never wanted to receive a Purple Heart.

I do not remember feeling pain from any of the wounds, not even when they were sewing me up.

Chapter 28

Organization, Tactics, and Jungle Warfare

An infantry company in battle should be about 160 men. This included two machine gun crews, 60 mm mortar crews, medics, and engineers used to blow things up. I was lucky to have more than eighty men total.

My company was organized into three rifle platoons. These platoons usually consisted of twenty-five to thirty men each, which included machine guns crews. In the jungle with the thick canopy overhead, we did not use the mortars, so we did not even carry them. We treated the jungle as if it was dark areas of poor visibility. This means that to move through the jungle we had to be organized, quiet, easily controlled, and alert. A point man was usually the first to go down the trail, followed within fifteen yards another man to cover the point man, and then a third man, all covering each other. Next would be their leader and the rest of the company. We all had to travel very, very quietly. Each and every man could jump up and down, and they wouldn't reveal any bumping or rattling. Vietnam was very hot, so most of us carried three canteens of water. Man-made sounds travel a long way when it's quiet.

My handle on the radio was Cheyenne 6. I've often heard it said that if you want to talk to Cheyenne, bump two canteens together. That would get my attention. My point man did not want anyone to know we were coming. Silence protected him.

Chapter 29

Patrolling and Booby Traps

When I first joined my unit, they had been pulling security duty around a headquarters unit. When we moved out on patrol in the rice paddies, our unit was divided into two patrols, thus creating two trails. That meant there were two men who could trip a booby trap. We patrolled about six hours and pulled into an area to spend the night. My unit had slept there before. Before I pulled into that area, I stopped my unit and sent two men to check for booby traps. I had learned that you do not sleep in the same area twice. Well, guess what! My two men found an old Vietcong papa-san who had been setting out a booby trap and had accidentally triggered it in the process. The papa-san was dead. After a good search of the area, we found no more booby traps.

When my men were finally preparing their positions for the night, I walked around to check their positions. A new man in country is called a cherry. As I walked the positions, I called out, "I check positions at night."

One of the old-timers called back, "I shoot anything that moves at night."

My answer was "I check positions with a M5, pin pulled." (An M5 is a hand grenade.)

Everybody froze and stopped what he was doing. Their looks said, "He ain't no cherry." The term *pin pulled* meant that if anything happened, I would throw a live grenade.

I did check the foxholes that night and found one of the guards looking into a four-foot-high bank of dirt. There was no way he could see anything. I asked him how far he could see. He stated he could see the mountains against the skyline. I told him I wasn't worried about the skyline. I was worried about the first thirty-five to forty feet. I was worried about an enemy crawling up close and throwing grenades into my sleeping people. These stories are 100 percent true.

In Vietnam we had two different enemies. One was the NVA, or North Vietnam Army, which was like any other army. The other was the Vietcong, commonly known as the VC. The VC were native Vietnamese who lived with the natives but were not loyal to the local governments. They were loyal to the communists of North Vietnam, dedicated to assist them by placing booby traps, threatening the locals, and doing anything else they could to help our enemies. They worked mostly undercover.

I have a multitude of stories like this. They are interesting to a point, so I'm going to continue to tell the stories for now. When you spend twenty-four months with about a hundred people in a jungle fighting a war, life does get interesting. By the way, we called the enemy *gooks* or *Charlie*. Alerting new troops, we used to sing a little ditty: "Down in the valley is a man called Charlie. When you get to know him, you call him Mr. Charles."

Chapter 30

A Shau Valley Landing

In early April 1968, we prepared to enter A Shau Valley. This was a part of Vietnam that the NVA considered to be their property. There had been no Americans in that valley for two years. To prepare for this mission, we were issued flak jackets, which were supposed to stop bullets, and practiced repelling out of helicopters by ropes.

There would be only six men to a helicopter, carrying extra food and ammunition. Each man also carried metal sticks used to stretch barbed wire where wire was needed. We were loaded on choppers that carried us over some high mountains, and we then dropped off the mountain down into the valley. Every bird that flew into the valley that day felt bullets.

I was sitting just behind the pilot when bullets came through the floor and hit the plastic canopy. A piece of flying canopy struck my pilot in the cheek. I reached to pull the plastic out of his cheek when I decided that I better not do that. The pilot brought the bird straight down into a daisy cutter bomb crater. A daisy cutter is a bomb with a long pipe on the nose of it. This pipe causes the bomb to explode before going deep into the ground, thus causing the bomb to cut down trees and shrubbery. This also creates a shallower bomb crater. We jumped out of the bird into the crater, and the pilot took off.

Chapter 31

A Shau Valley, Jungle Combat

As soon as the pilot cleared the area, we took up positions to protect ourselves. I had already decided that I would use the least wounded to carry the wounded to take up defensive positions, expecting the enemy to show up rather quickly. No enemy showed up. We immediately started digging foxholes, while some guards were watching for the enemy to come up the hill. The Vietnamese did not want us to be where we were.

One of my men called me to come over to his foxhole. He wanted to show me something. I went over there. There was a five hundred-pound bomb that had been dropped from the skies. It had penetrated the top of a ridge, and as it fell, the bomb turned and was sticking out of the side of the ridge. The Vietnamese had been chiseling the nose off the bomb; there were chisel marks to show this. And my man had been digging his foxhole right beside of the bomb.

Things were quiet after that until darkness. A Shau Valley must have been about a mile wide and more than twenty miles long. We were on the hill looking down into the valley. I think later they changed the name to LZ Cecil.

There were lots of Vietnamese still in the valley, including trucks, weapons, and stored supplies. Our helicopters must have pulled sixty to eighty missions that day, carrying men and supplies and dropping them on an old airstrip left by the French years earlier. The American units were digging in and stretching trip flares plus Claymore mines around their guard positions. As soon as dark set in, the Vietnamese started their engines and began driving real tanks out of the valley. Several American units started shooting flares high in the sky, lighting up the whole countryside. These flares would pop open, and small parachutes would cause the flares to float gently to the ground. When the flares lit up, these tanks sped up, and when the flares burned out, the tanks slowed down. It was reported the exact opposite way. *No way.* When the flares lit up, the tanks sped up. They were driving under our lights. *I was there.* Sometimes I get a little heated up when reporters do not know what they're talking about. The big deal was that our surprise attack had worked.

Over the next several days, American forces captured vehicles, supplies, weapons, and prisoners. My unit captured more than 1,100 Chinese rifles, which had been dug out of tunnels.

We were taken off LZ *Cecil* and were put to following the tracks of the tanks that had driven out of the valley. We came up upon a tank that was flipped upside down. I never did figure out why that tank was upside down on level ground. I crawled into the upside down tank and found gas masks and tin cans of meat. The gas masks told me that they were prepared for chemical warfare.

After I crawled out of that tank, we proceeded to follow the tank tracks. Eventually, we came upon an enemy motor pool area. It was just an open area with indications that it had been a motor pool. There were no vehicles in sight. I was pulled away before we found any vehicles. The 1,100 rifles were taken and stored at our rear area. Every man who left our battalion was supposed to be able to take one home with him. My son has mine. It's a Chinese-made SK-44 with a folding bayonet.

Chapter 32

Patrolling, Security, and Getting Wounded

We were brought back to the Phu Loi airstrip where we were assigned as security to the people at the airstrip. When the unit who had been providing the security went to pick up their flares, they tripped one of them.

During the time we had been patrolling the valley, flying boxcars had been passing over the airfield and dropping parachutes of artillery ammunition on pallets. Some of these pallets had missed the airstrip and fell into four-foot-high elephant grass. The tripped flare started burning, which caught other things on fire, including the elephant grass and then the pallets.

I passed the word all over the strip to take cover, because the pallet of ammunition was going to blow up. My radio operator and I crawled into a bunker. I stood up in the door the bunker to confirm that everyone had taken cover. Naturally, I spotted one of my men who had not gotten the word. He was outside of his bunker up blowing his air mattress.

I yelled, "Bivona." He didn't hear me, so I yelled again. He still did not hear me. I bent over to pick up my M-16 rifle. I was going to shoot over his head to send him to his bunker. The moment I bent over, the pallet of ammunition blew up. A large fragment of metal hit me in my right hip, taking out a hunk of meat the size of my hand. If I had not had bent over, the fragment of metal would have gotten me right in the gut. My angel up there was taking care of me. There was absolutely no pain.

I showed my bloody hand to my radio operator, Larry Potts. I picked up the mike on my radio and called my company commander, Captain Tillitt. I told him that when an explosion took place, I had been hit in the butt and would have to be medevaced to receive treatment.

I climbed aboard a helicopter with four wounded enemy soldiers who appeared to be drugged unconscious. When we reached a MASH (mobile army surgical hospital), a doctor asked me if I was in pain, and I said no. He informed me to go into the mess hall and get something to eat while he took care of others.

When I walked into that mess hall, I saw cucumbers floating in vinegar. Tears rolled out of my eyes and down my cheeks, and I just let them roll. I had been eating out of cans for weeks—C rations. Cucumbers got to me.

Later, a doctor had me lie down on my stomach on the operating table. Within three minutes, he had me sewn up and told me he was done. This was two hours after I'd been hit, and still there was no pain. This was unreal. I lay around the hospital for a couple of days and returned to my unit with stitches in my butt. And I say again: All of the above is 100 percent true. Unbelievable but true.

Chapter 33

Getting Sniper and Flank Security

A couple of days later my unit got into trouble in the jungle. I went by the aid station, had the stitches removed, gathered my gear, hopped on a bird, and joined my unit in the field. When the bird landed on top of a hill, I joined my unit. I got a welcome from my troops and asked for the CO (commanding officer) Captain Tillitt. Someone pointed down the hill, so I headed that way. Shortly, I came upon my CO with his back against a small tree.

He turned around, looked up at me, and said, "Where did you come from?"

"Off that bird," I answered.

Just like John Wayne, I had rejoined my unit.

A few days later we were moving down the trail when one of my men shot a sniper out of the tree. After he had crashed to the ground, I walked over and started searching his pockets and found some North Vietnamese paper money. I passed it out to all the people who were there and suggested they write on each bill: "Taken from a sniper shot of out of tree in A Shau Valley. May 4, 1968." I think my grandson in Las Vegas ended up with mine.

One day we were moving down a trail and another trail came in from the right. I told one of my squad leaders to send two men down the trail about fifty yards. I didn't want the enemy to walk up on us from my right flank. About the same time my point man spotted a Vietnamese soldier about the same time the enemy spotted him. The Vietnamese soldier grabbed his rifle and ran off to the right. It just so happened that he ran between the two men on the other trail. The second man shot and killed the enemy. He was a new man who had been with me five days.

Chapter 34

Point Man Pinned Down

At that time I was thirty-six years old, and most of my men were eighteen or nineteen years old. When anything happened in front of the column, the call would come back, "Cheyenne forward." When I got to the front of the column, the only thing between me and the enemy was hot air. It did not take me long to ask why. That time the answer was that the point man had found a Ho Chi Minh slick track in a mud puddle and muddy water was still running into the footprint. I did not need to come up front and watch muddy water run into a footprint.

By the way, a Ho Chi Minh slick was a sandal cut from a tire with thongs tied to it. This was what the NVA and VC soldiers used for shoes.

One day we were going down the trail and … *bang, bang, bang.* Shots were fired. Here it came. "Cheyenne forward."

"Why?" I asked.

"Your point man is pinned down," I was told.

This meant he had been fired at, hit the ground, and was scared to get up. I took off running up the trail, followed by my radio operator Larry Potts. We came to a big tree lying across the trail with five of my men behind the tree.

I called out, "Where is he?"

One man pointed toward eleven o'clock.

I yelled out, "Are you okay?"

He yelled back, "They shot my canteen."

"Stay there," I told him. "I'll get you out."

I was going to use tactics that I had taught in many classes. It was called fire and movement. One man shoots while another man moves. When moving to politically correct, it was changed to fire and maneuver. I tried it, and it worked.

I called for machine guns up. I placed one machine gun three yards to my right and the other machine gun three yards to my left. I told both of them that when I said, "Commence firing," to alternate four-round bursts. There were three men with M-16 rifles. I told two of them to start firing slow fire and the other to count off eight or ten rounds and then start firing while the others reloaded.

"Everybody, see that big tree right in front of us? Shoot to the right of it. I'm going to bring the point man around to my left," I yelled. "When we open up, face my voice and bear a little to your right for ten or fifteen yards and come over to me where I am. Everybody! Shoot low and throw rocks and gravel in their faces. Commence firing!"

And everybody did. The point man crawled up to my left side.

"Cease fire!" I called out.

Everybody did. I looked at the point man, and his britches were wet. I said, "You look like you peed your britches."

His answer was "Dammit. I told you that they shot my canteen."

I saved his life, and he got mad at me. I have not mentioned his name, because I can't remember his name. To complete this story, I must tell you that when we were lying behind that log, the Vietnamese were throwing hand grenades over our heads. The first grenade I saw looked like a Chinese concussion grenade. It looked like it was made of metal with a wooden handle and a string hanging out the back.

Larry Potts, my radio operator, was beside of me during all of this. Later we agreed that the Vietnamese threw between three and seven grenades over our heads. We cannot remember even one of those grenades exploding. And that's not all ... There is more.

Potts grabbed a grenade and pulled the pin while yelling, "I'll get them. I'll get them." Potts then threw the grenade up in the air where it hit a tree limb and fell back to on the other side of the log we were behind. Potts grabbed another grenade, pulled the pin, threw the grenade, and it did the same as the first grenade. It hit the same tree limb and fell back on the other side of the log we were behind.

That's when I said, "No more grenades, Potts."

All of this is 100 percent true. I have witnesses. My angel was certainly busy that day.

Chapter 35

Thirty–Minute Combat Assault

A couple of days later we were patrolling through four-foot-high elephant grass when I got a call to return to my command post (CP) and prepare for a Charlie Alpha (combat assault). That meant that helicopters were on the way to pick us up for an attack somewhere. Just as we got back to the CP, I could see the helicopters coming for us. At the same time, somebody gave me two new men. I gave them to the leader of my first squad, telling them to stay with him until this was over. The choppers landed when we immediately climbed aboard.

What was happening was that an officer had been flying in a helicopter and had spotted a group of NVA soldiers sitting off the trail eating a meal. This officer called for artillery fire on top of these enemy soldiers, who scattered in every direction. The officer then called for the Charlie Alpha on the spot where the NVA soldiers had been.

The choppers landed—we landed—and started making a circle for defense. Our training had taught us that the first squad landing, using the clock system, would spread his men from ten o'clock to two o'clock. The second squad would cover from two o'clock to six o'clock. The third squad covered from six o'clock to ten o'clock. This gets protection in a 360-degree a circle.

We had just recently gotten to A Shau Valley, and we were all still wearing flak jackets. On the command to move out, all the men moved forward, making the circle larger, and more birds landed, bringing more soldiers. We knew we were looking for the enemy; however, just outside our circle was a clump of trees. Naturally, those men walked around that clump of trees.

Two enemy soldiers with rifles jumped out of the trees. I brought my rifle up to shoot them. Captain Tillitt and his radio operators were between me and the enemy. I could not shoot, but they did. The NVA soldiers wounded two of my men before they were killed by my men. The wounded were wearing flak jackets and were both shot in left shoulders and lower-right bodies below the flak jackets. They were both taken to MASH units.

When I first got off the choppers there, I could see a 150-yard-high, rather steep hill. To the left side of that hill was two-foot-high dead grass. To the right side of the hill was forest. My first squad had gone into the forest looking for enemy soldiers when there came a helicopter with someone pulling pins out of grenades and throwing them down into the trees on to my first squad. Nobody was hurt. My angel was still taking care of us. Good job!

Chapter 36

Enough before Supper

The operation was called off, so the choppers come back, picked us up, and took us to our original CP. When we unloaded from the birds and they had taken off, I saw our new men and busted out laughing. In their first thirty minutes with me, they had been in a combat assault, seen two men wounded, run into the woods chasing enemy soldiers, had hand grenades dropped on them, were picked up by choppers, and were brought home safely. That's about enough before supper.

I did tell them it would probably be six months before we did something like that again. Tsk-tsk. I hate to ask you to believe this, but each and every word is true. And I did leave some stuff out.

Chapter 37

Getting Food and Water

When we first came into A Shau Valley at LZ *Cecil*, we carried water and food to last a couple of days. In just a few days, both were gone. My men were becoming hungry and thirsty. I picked one man to go with me, and we went outside of the perimeter. Using the man as security to watch out for Charlie, I walked down the hill from my men's foxholes. There, I found cans of C rations. I picked up an armload of food as we went back inside the perimeter.

As I walked between the foxholes, my men asked, "Where did you find that?"

My answer was "This is all the food you threw away the day we got here. Squad leaders, make sure you put out security before you send people down to gather food."

Later, I got another man and a couple of machetes. I do not know why I picked up the machetes. I didn't usually use them. At any rate, my security and I went out of the perimeter, going uphill. After a couple hundred yards, we came upon some bamboo vines. I took a machete and cut a vine in two above a knuckle. When I tipped the bamboo cane, water came pouring out—not much, maybe a half an ounce, but it was water. Taking turns watching for Charlie, my man and I drank water, filled our canteens, and went downhill to the perimeter. As we walked between the foxholes, I poured water out of my canteen. Shocked, men asked where we got the water.

I told them and then ended by saying, "Squad leaders, make sure you put out the security before anyone gets water."

I don't remember ever learning how to get water from a bamboo vine. My angel was still with me.

M-16 rifles have a selector that lets you go from bang-bang-bang to automatic, da-da-da-da-da. When moisture got around a selector, it would freeze up. When we awoke in the morning, I would remind my men to point their rifles to the sky and check their selectors. One morning after a heavy dew, four or five of my men got excited, because their selectors were frozen. I warned them to be careful, get out that little plastic bottle of the oil they had been carrying, and put one drop on their selector. This made the selector work. They thought this was magic.

Chapter 38

O'Shea's Coffee and the Hole in His Picture

One afternoon we moved into a large, empty cornfield that had not been used in several years. That day, out of the jungle, we dug foxholes and slept the night. The next morning my platoon was to be the last to move out, so my men took their time eating and making their coffee. When the leading platoon moved into the jungle, Charlie opened up with machine guns and mortars.

My men dove into the foxholes, knowing that when bullets are flying, Charlie will run through the foxholes and pitch explosives into them. I was in a foxhole looking around. My men were in the holes with steel helmets on their heads; it looked like a field full of turtles. I told Larry Potts to take a look at this. One of my men named O'Shea had been making a canteen cup of Malaysian coffee, a mixture of C ration coffee and chocolate. With bullets flying, O'Shea jumped out of his foxhole, ran, picked up his cup of coffee, and then got back into his foxhole. I wonder if he spilled any of his coffee.

One day we were going down a trail in the jungle when Charlie started shooting at us. We dove for the ground. When O'Shea hit the ground, his steel pot (helmet) fell off, and a bullet went through the top of his helmet. Inside of his helmet was his girlfriend's picture. O'Shea took one look at the bullet hole in his girlfriend's picture, jumped up, and took off running down the trail, cussing and firing both left and right as he yelled. That's an Irish man for you. He did not get hurt. There's my angel again.

Chapter 39

Finding Painkillers

Captain Tillitt and I both knew that if you were on the high ground, you may run into enemy trail watchers. We also knew that if we went down to the water, we would find Charlie. One day when we woke up, Captain Tillitt asked me what I wanted to do for the day. I said it had been quiet for a few days, so we needed to tighten up the troops. We went downhill to the water. Charlie had moved out. However, we found cases of painkiller. I put out the word to not destroy the painkillers. We left it where we found it in consideration for the enemy. No one argued with me. Thanks.

Chapter 40

July 24, 1968

I was not present during the next events, so what I say here is hearsay.

My unit was in the jungle, and I was up on LZ *Carol*, approximately a mile to a mile and a half from my unit. This mile and a half was up and down steep, thick jungle mountains. There was no way I could get to my unit. It was the equivalent of twenty miles with no roads back home; plus, this was with Charlie.

This portion of my story is related by Art Jacobs and Peter O'Sullivan, the pilots of the medevac birds who tried to get the wounded away from Charlie.

This section includes a firsthand account on the medical evacuations of many critically wounded Bravo Company troopers on July 24, 1968. The story is based on information received from the pilot who actually conducted some of these evacuations. I hope that this gripping story will prompt those of you who were involved in this action to come forward with additional information.

The brave crews of medical evacuation (medevac) helicopters, commonly known as dustoffs and medevacs, were often required to perform heroic feats when evacuating wounded combat troopers. However, there was an important difference between a dustoff and a medevac. The Forty-Fourth Medical Brigade was responsible for dustoff operations for all the divisions in Vietnam with the notable exception of the First Cav Division.

The First Cav Division had a dedicated medevac capability directly under their control for very good reasons: they had faster reaction times, crews were familiar with our concept of operating, and it fostered a closer bond with First Cav Division crews evacuating their "own" troops. The Fifteenth Medical Battalion provided direct medical support to First Cav Division units, and this included the aerial evacuation services provided by the Medevac Platoon, consisting of twenty-four pilots and twelve aircraft.

For Bravo Company troopers, it was extremely important to know that a medevac would always come when needed, and this frequently involved precarious missions at night from locations deep in the jungle and during intense firefights. As the requirement for a medevac was usually the result of hostile actions, most evacuations were conducted under extremely hazardous conditions, and we greatly admired the courage and dedication of our medevac crews.

The primary evacuation helicopter used by the First Cav Division was a specially equipped Huey designed to carry three stretcher patients or six walking wounded. A medevac crew consisted of the aircraft commander, copilot, crew chief, door gunner, and a medic. During some missions, gunships provided protection for a medevac. Although most dustoffs were unarmed, the First Cav Division medevacs carried two M-60 machine guns for defensive purposes only. (The crew chief manned the other M-60.) The Red Cross on a medevac Huey did not provide them with immunity, and many were shot down. Consequently, when we were in desperate need of resupply, they were known to drop off critical supplies and ammo to us, referred to by one pilot as preventive medicine.

In response to our request for a medevac, the pilot would contact us by radio, announcing that he was inbound and request that we pop smoke as he approached our location. This triggered an exchange on the correct smoke color, as our enemy also tried to mislead medevac pilots and lure them to other locations with the use of smoke grenades. As we frequently sustained casualties in jungle or mountainous terrain, suitable landing zones were not always available, and a hoist system was used to retrieve wounded soldiers from these locations. As the Huey hovered over the jungle pickup location, the medic would lower a litter or jungle penetrator (a folded seat with a harness) to the Bravo Company troopers on the ground. The wounded troopers would be strapped into these devices by a qualified person, usually the platoon medic, and hoisted up. During the flight to the treatment facility or clearing station, the crew medic would administer first aid using the medical supplies and equipment that he had in the cabin for this purpose.

On July 24–25, 1968, Bravo Company was conducting search-and-destroy operations in a jungle and mountainous area west of Hue. Not much is known about the details, except that Bravo had a fierce firefight with a large enemy force and suffered thirteen KIAs (killed in action) and many wounded during this two-day period. Evacuating our casualties was a major problem not only for Bravo troopers, but also for the medevac crews.

Here is a firsthand account prepared by Aircraft Commander Art Jacobs, who conducted three aborted medevac missions on July 24, 1968. Art's call sign was Medevac 21, and he remembers talking on the radio to Eager Arms 26 India, Blackfoot Platoon.

> On our first attempt, we took all kinds of hits coming in on the approach. My copilot was slightly wounded (shrapnel in the arm where a bullet had hit the side of my seat), and our door gunner was shot in the head (he remains 100 percent disabled and

in a wheelchair to this day). We had our engine oil temperature and engine oil pressure lights come on from the hits and had no choice but to go back to Evans.

On our second attempt, we actually got to a hover and got one of your guys up. But just as the hoist got to the skids, all hell broke loose. Your wounded guy was hit in the hand, our crew chief was hit in the leg with shrapnel from the bullets coming through the floor, and we lost our hydraulics. Again, we had no choice but to return to Evans, and I was worried that we wouldn't make it because we also had fuel pouring out the bottom.

After losing the second aircraft, we were told that there was now a moratorium on making any future rescue attempts and that a ground unit would try to get the wounded to a landing zone. An hour later, your Battalion Commander (Lt. Comm. John Gibney) showed up at our company area asking for volunteers to fly out there again. I was terribly impressed with how concerned and impassioned he was. He said, "My boys really need your help. The WIAs will become KIAs if you cannot go." There was *no way* we would turn him down, and I went looking for another aircraft and crew.

On the third attempt, I had a whole new crew, and we were about to lower the hoist when they opened up again. I was shot in the arm, gave the controls to my copilot, and told him to hold our position. Just then, about seven or eight warning lights came on, including the dreaded Engine Chip

Detector light. We started climbing out and banking to the left (west), but we were still taking hits. We continued our turn, and then the engine quit. At first, we headed to a low spot in the valley, but then we saw a small clearing no bigger than the helicopter. Somehow we managed to plunk the Huey into that one spot. About a half hour later there were gunships overhead, and they called in one of our other Medevac birds ... None too soon, because the gunships started taking fire from what they said were bad guys coming toward us.

I was evacuated to Japan and did not return to my unit until September. Shortly after my return to LZ *Sharon*, someone from Bravo 2/8th came over and gave me a captured Chinese bolt-action rifle, which I still have in my study today.

As a small token of our appreciation for his heroic deeds on 7/24/68, we have made Art Jacobs an Honorary Member of Eager Arms. Prepared by Art Jacobs and Peter O'Sullivan.

To Honor Our Fallen and Wounded Heroes

Art Jacobs and the members of Bravo Company wish to honor the following crew members who participated in the Medevac operations on 24 July 1968:

SP4 John Alling, Crew Chief. Killed when his helicopter was shot down on 26 November 1968.

1LT Stephen Beals, Pilot. Killed when his helicopter was shot down on 26 November 1968.

SP4 Jerry Dick, Door Gunner, severely wounded
during the Medevac on 24
July, and 100% disabled.

Banty Rooster is back again.

On the morning of July 24, my unit got into a firefight with Charlie, throwing grenades and shooting at each other. The end result was eight dead and six of our troops wounded. We lost three medevac helicopters that day due to wounded crew members and enemy damage.

I have been told that we only had twelve medevac birds in North Vietnam at that time, and we had just lost three of them, leaving nine. The end result was fourteen dead and many wounded to be carried out of the jungle up to LZ *Carol*. Another unit was dispatched to meet my unit and assist in carrying the dead and wounded. I met them two days later when they came to LZ *Carol*. My men were totally exhausted, weak, and hungry. They didn't have much food for several days. It took more than a week for them to recover after that ordeal before we went back to war.

To add to that same story: In late September, one of my platoons were moving on a dirt road to set up an ambush to catch enemy movement. A Vietcong squeezed down on a Claymore firing device, throwing more than a thousand half-inch ball bearings into the middle of the platoon, killing one and wounding thirteen. I was not with them, however, I was listening on the radio. I could hear what was going on when a medevac helicopter came to pick up the wounded. It was about ten thirty at night.

When I heard the chopper pilot's voice, I recognized it as the voice of the same man who had lost three helicopters two months before: Art Jacobs. Not being with the troops, there was nothing I could do. I couldn't even talk to him, because it would interfere with them doing their job. The next day I got one of the 1,100 rifles that we had captured and gave it to one of my men, asking him to clean it up for me. I walked up to our aid station and asked somebody where the medevac bird pilots stayed. I walked into the indicated tent and found three very young-looking young men.

I asked, "Which one of you were picking up my men in the rice paddies last night?"

One of the young men indicated it was him. I walked over and presented him with a bolt-action Chinese rifle with a folding bayonet, saying, "Thanks from Company B, Second of the Eighth."

The question is: If I was not present around the company on July 24, 1968, how could I recognize Art Jacobs' voice two months later? I do not understand.

Chapter 41

Cherry School, Firing during Night Attacks

We had six more KIAs within the next twenty days. Sometime around late October my unit moved from the mountains to the rice paddies of South Vietnam. I did not go south, as I was reassigned to teach at Cherry School.

Cherry School was where we sent new arrivals into Vietnam to be taught what expect in the country. They became acquainted with new equipment, weapons, tactics, booby traps, and the like. during their first five days in the cavalry. Their night training included being put in a foxhole and firing at a target twenty-five yards away. This target was about the size of a case of beer standing on end. It was an empty ammunition box taken from jet aircraft, which made of a metal that created a flash when hit by a bullet. The shooter could see these targets when lights were on and could only fire at the target after the lights had been turned off for two minutes. The shooter learned to search for the target and shoot low. Ricochets counted. Once they had actually hit a target and it made the flash, the shooter had learned how to defend himself in night attacks. When you can't see the target, the tendency is to shoot too high.

Chapter 42

Coming Home

I stayed at the Cherry School until late January. That's when I became a short-timer preparing to come home. I had received orders to Fort Gordon, Georgia, with a thirty-day leave of absence. I flew from Vietnam to Japan to the United States. I arrived in Columbia, South Carolina, on February 5, 1969, with two wars under my belt.

My wife of seventeen years and three children, ages fourteen, fifteen, and sixteen, picked me up at the airport. One hour later, I hugged my wife and said, "Still love me?"

Her answer was "No. I want a divorce."

After discussing the situation for three days, I agreed to the divorce. She agreed to give me the house that was nearly paid for, and I agreed to pay support for the children. I decided since South Carolina was only one hundred miles from my assignment at Fort Gordon, Georgia, I did not need to be in the same town as my divorced wife. I realized people fall in love, and they fall out of love. There's no need for fighting. That just hurts the kids. After a couple of days, I packed my bags and reported to Fort Gordon, canceled my leave, and reported to work.

In time of war, God adored and soldier knighted. War is over, danger past, God ignored, and soldier slighted.

Some of my children stayed with me off and on for the next few years. They got married as time passed. My wife notified me that our divorce was final. By then, I was dating my present wife. One day we were walking down a dirt road, and I made the comment that for nickel I would marry her. When we got home, she gave me the nickel … So I married her and her two children, who were five and six years old. That gave me a total of five kids.

A few years later my ex-wife passed away due to cancer. I am very close to my children. They are all older than fifty now, all self-sufficient, and do not ask for money. You can't do any better than that.

Chapter 43

Army Retirement and Getting a Driver's Job

Let's talk about my small businesses. I bought a restaurant in a great location, rebuilt it, redesigned it, paved the parking lot, renamed it, and opened up. It was an immediate success. I had hired a manager with restaurant experience, a cook who made wonderful pancakes, and two intelligent, friendly waitresses.

Within ten days, my manager called the cook the N-word. My pancakes immediately went lousy. When I learned what had happened, I took the manager outside and told him that he was not ready to be a manager, fired him, and gave the cook a raise. It took a while to get the business back up, and then I sold it and bought a laundromat that was in a good location. I redesigned, renamed it, and bought a total of twelve washing machines, including large washing machines, as well as four large gas dryers. Business increased. I had three ladies running the laundromat, working six-hour shifts and dividing the shifts to make seven-day weeks. Everyone was happy, and business was good. Ladies who needed the money could work more hours. Ladies who did not need the money could work fewer hours. Later, I sold this business and bought a bar (saloon).

In business, when you have other people handling your money.

they get sticky fingers. *Don't forget that.* I set up a system that allowed me to catch sticky fingers. I did all of this while still driving the eighteen-wheeler truck, which made me a very busy man.

I redesigned the bar, making an extra-high U-shaped bar, and added two pool tables, booths, a jukebox, and a dance floor. I also paved the parking lot. The bar was located just outside an army base gate and just off a busy highway.

Thinking about sticky fingers, I went to the bar one morning and put a small pencil mark on the height of the alcohol in my whiskey bottles. I then placed the whiskey bottles with all the labels facing out, so I could tell when the bottles had been moved. At the end of the night, I was there when the bar closed. After collecting the day's money intake from the cash register, I could tell how much of what was sold.

One of the waitresses was giving her boyfriend free drinks. Knowing what brand he drank, I checked that whiskey bottle. The alcohol level in the bottle was an inch and a half lower than my pencil mark. I showed both of them that I knew what was going on. She needed the money bad, as she had children to support, and the boyfriend was not a good catch. She was looking for a husband. I told the man he was not allowed in my bar again, and I told her that she had a choice to make—stay with me or stay with him. She stayed working for me. Good riddance!

One evening a twenty-one-year-old punk came into my bar and sat down on a barstool to drink. A short time later, he called one of my waitresses a bitch. Oops! He shouldn't have done that.

I walked over to him, put my belly about six inches from his nose, and asked my bartender for a bottle of beer. There I stood, chugalugging that bottle of beer till it was gone. My belly was still six inches from his nose.

I stepped back and looked him straight in the eye and said, "I am fifty-eight years old. I have been around, and I do not know if I have AIDS or not, but I am getting ready to puke all over you."

That punk jumped up and ran out the door, yelling, "That man is crazy." Then he jumped in his car and left town. This prevented the blue lights from being parked in front of my bar, which is not good advertising. That punk never did come back.

One evening a customer poured a mixed drink on the head of my bartender, soaking her and all her clothes. She grabbed a cue stick and started beating him over the head with it. He ducked and crawled under a pool table. I took the cue stick from her and told the man to leave and to ask for permission before he came back. He owed her an apology. No blue lights again.

I spent the next couple of years looking for what I wanted to do. I worked as a salesman, among other things. With that behind me, I got into a new life. I became an over-the-road big rig truck driver. My job was to deliver golf carts to golf courses in all forty-eight states plus Canada. To be a well-paid, year-round tourist was a dream come true.

I was given a new truck with my name on the door. The weight when loaded was seventy-two thousand pounds, or thirty-six tons. Normal freight haulers load weight was eighty thousand pounds, or forty tons. They were harder to drive and harder to stop.

I had a specially built trailer designed to carry thirty golf carts. The trailer had three decks; one was a normal trailer deck, and then four feet above that was another top deck whose height could be adjusted by an electric winch. Each deck held twelve golf carts. There was another set of decks beneath the trailer that held six golf carts for a total of thirty golf carts. When you open the trailer doors there was a ramp that could be raised or lowered by another electric winch. Golf carts could be loaded or unloaded by simply driving the golf carts on or off the ramp. It was perfect—a one-man deal.

Chapter 44

Life on the Road

I spent the next twenty-four years driving all up and down and all around the forty-eight states and Canada. I've had peanut butter on my waffles in Portland, Oregon. I've had breakfast in Tijuana, Mexico, been off the tip of Florida so far that I had the Gulf of Mexico on one side of my road and the Atlantic Ocean on the other, and been on the beaches of Maine where you dig clams.

I retired from driving the big rig in 2005 at seventy-five years of age. My company would send me for a physical several times a year to protect the company in case of an accident. Personally, I fully believe that I had driven on every mile of interstate in the United States at that date. I am sure other interstates have been built since then. My company bought me a new truck every four years. My trucks had air-bag suspension, which made for a smooth ride. It was wonderful.

Truck drivers are just one big happy family with our CB radios. You never turn anyone down when asked for help. In those years, from 1981 to 2005, if a truck driver saw a four-wheeler, or any other vehicle, sitting on the side of the road, we would stop to check the problem. In those days, if you had a problem and told a truck driver, he would help take care of it. Truck drivers had an excellent reputation. We chatted on those CB radios, reporting the location of highway patrol cruisers looking for speeders and traffic jams, spreading gossip, and swapping humorous stories.

After a couple of years, my children were graduating from school, growing up, dating, and starting to live their own lives. My second wife was working and quite busy. My job required me to deliver my load somewhere on this earth and return home with an empty truck. They did not want me to use time seeking a load because we were busy delivering more than a hundred thousand golf carts per year, anywhere and everywhere at thirty golf carts per load. It just so happens that golf courses are open in the spring, summer, and fall. This means that in winter, they wanted to replace old golf carts with new golf carts, thus having us drivers traveling through snow, ice, and cold weather, making every trip a challenge—nothing wrong with that.

Chapter 45

My Backyard, United States

I call the territory of the United States my backyard, and I love her. The following are some of the events that occurred while driving those twenty-four years.

One night I was eastbound in Wyoming when a westbound driver called out on his CB radio that eastbound drivers were running into a whiteout. That means high winds and heavy snow that is so bad you can't see the road.

I called back, "No I'm not."

"Yes you are," he replied.

"No I am not," I insisted.

"Why not?" the other trucker asked.

"Because I'm getting off at this truck stop in front of me and going to sleep," I responded. "Bye."

One day I was heading west from Denver, Colorado, going into the Rocky Mountains. My loaded truck would slow down going up steep hills and speed up going down hills. Two young ladies in a station wagon passed me going uphill, and I winked at the passenger who told the driver what I did. I passed them going down a steep hill. The next time I came to a downhill stretch, I unbuttoned my shirt, and on the uphill I pulled my shirt up and flashed them with my booby. You should have seen those ladies removing blouses and unhooking bras. They were laughing and flashing on the next uphill. We were just passing the time.

I was to deliver to a farm north of Winnipeg, Canada. When I arrived at the farm, I was told to unload at a barn. They had removed the snow so I could go into the barnyard, turn around, and back up to the barn. The temperature was twenty degrees below zero. I looked at the situation and decided it would be colder in the morning, so I proceeded to unload. I had a heavy apron that I wore backward because of the cold seats. By the way, I had to use my zippo cigarette lighter to melt ice from the switches to get the keys in the switch. I unloaded that night and went to sleep. The next morning they signed the papers, and I headed back to Georgia.

Another time three trucks showed up at the same time at a golf course in Tucson, Arizona. It took half a day to unload and reload all three trucks with used golf carts. It was 110 degrees at the time we finished. I have been in Needles, California, when the temperature was 110 degrees by eight o'clock in the morning. You walk fast going across parking lots with hot pavement.

I had a load of golf carts to deliver to a golf course north of Missoula, Montana. I was following directions to the golf course when I started driving up a mountain. It wasn't a very steep mountain, but it was a mountain that kept going up and up and up. I came to some golden wheat fields, stretching for acres and acres and acres— not a telephone pole or a ranch house in sight, just golden wheat as far as the eye could see. After a while, I picked up my CB mike and said, "Hello, God."

From somewhere out of the heavens, an answer came back. "Yes, Son?"

I surmised that it could be another truck driver somewhere. Or God. Other than that, the airways were completely silent.

Chapter 46

Lost Girls

My wife and I had a friend who was the divorced mother of two attractive daughters, twelve and fourteen years of age. One night I came home from a trip from the West Coast at about two thirty in the morning. As soon as I came in the door, the phone rang. It was the mother of the daughters.

She explained that the girls had been missing for two days, and she was sick with worry. She asked if there was anything I could do. I asked about her daughters girlfriends. She told me no one knew anything. Then I asked about boyfriends. No, she had one, but they had broken up.

Being that was the only lead I had, I pushed the issue. What was his name, and where did he live? Mama gave me his name and said he was a soldier. I told Mama that I would try and hung up. I immediately called the Army Post Locater, gave the operator his name, and got his address. I then got in my car and drove to his army base at four thirty in the morning.

I found his living quarters where one of his friends told me that the ex-boyfriend's parents were in town, and he was in a motel with them. I learned that he was required to be at roll call at six in the morning and that he drove a red car. There I was, a fifty-five-year-old retired first sergeant in civilian clothes. When the soldier drove into the parking lot, I walked over to him and told him to follow me, which he did. I took him to the unit commander's office, where I briefed the CO as to what was going on. The CO asked the young man what was going on, and he denied any knowledge of anything.

After a few minutes, the CO turned to me and stated, "First Sergeant, I don't believe he knows anything."

My answer was "May I?"

I walked over to young man, stared him in the eye her for about twenty seconds, and said, "The mother is not going to press charges. She just wants her daughters back. If I walk out of here this morning thinking you don't know anything and later I find that you know where they are, I will not call the police. I will take care of you myself."

The young man turned to the CO and said, "Sir, may I start over?"

My next question was "Where are they?"

He gave me a motel name and room number. I then told the person in charge to put a guard on the man so that he had no opportunity to call the girls, because I knew they would run. Just as I got to the motel room, the twelve-year-old came outside, got some cookies from a machine, and then saw me. She got so shaky she couldn't get the key in the lock, so I had to open the door for her.

That's when the fourteen-year-old started yelling that she was not going to go home. I told her that was okay, but if she didn't do what I said, there would be lots of blue lights outside. The police would take to jail and lock her up, and she would have a police record for the rest of her life. I picked up the room phone, called their mother, and told her I had her daughters. She could pick them up at my house.

Driving to my house and waiting for their mother gave me

time to get the fourteen-year-old's excuses and story. She said she was pregnant, among other things. I asked how she knew she was pregnant, and she told me that she had been to the health department. She even gave me the address.

My thirteen-year-old daughter heard all of this and motioned for me to come down the hall. She then whispered to me that the Health Department had moved and gave me a different address.

When the mother arrived, I brought her up to date, stating that the girl was lying through her teeth, saying she was pregnant and didn't know that the Health Department had moved to a different address. Later the girls told their mother that if they ever decided to run away again, they would tell me first. I never did ask my thirteen-year-old daughter how she knew where the Health Department was.

I have no idea why I did not believe the young soldier. I had no indication that he was not telling the truth. ESP? Extrasensory perception? I had ESP many times during my time in the wars.

Chapter 47

How I Wrote This Book

Because of my awesome life, many people have been urging me to write this book. For the past few years, I have been keeping notes about my memories and incidents that have come to mind. When I was fifteen years old, I could type fifty to fifty-five words per minute. Seventy years later, I am not that good. However, I came across this program called Dragon NaturallySpeaking, Version 13. You can buy it most anywhere for $99.99. You can find it on sale for $49.99. This includes earphone and a microphone, as well as a CD to install it on your computer.

Then you sit with your keyboard and monitor in front of you. Click the red button on top of your screen, and it will turn green. Anything you say will be typed on your computer. You can delete anything you want, make corrections, and alter anything you have said. This is what's called a KISS situation—keep it simple, sweetie.

Chapter 48

Things to Ponder

Things to ponder. Here are some things I have learned, to give you something to think about and for you to consider using. The following are little known but are suggested:

If you ever see a dog that is losing his hair so much that the bare skin shows, this may be a disease called mange, which is caused by mites digging deep into the skin. This causes intense itching and scratching, resulting in the loss of hair. If you coat the entire dog with burned motor oil from your car, it will suffocate the mites in just a couple of hours, stopping the scratching. Bathe the dog with Dawn dish soap to dissolve all the oil, and in a few weeks, the dog will have a new beautiful fur coat.

If you want to join the US Army, start exercising and running to prepare your body for basic training. For the first couple of months, you will experience so much physical training that it will tire you out and make you so fatigued that it will be harder for you to learn and perform to your utmost. Being in the US Army is wonderful way to move into adulthood. All your needs are provided without worry about money. By the time you finish your first tour, you should be grown up.

A few years ago I had a swimming pool in my backyard. My

five-year-old granddaughter loved the shallow end of the pool and was allowed to spend too much time in the hot sun. Soon she was crying because of a sunburn. I went into my house and got a jar of mayonnaise from the refrigerator, which was already cool. Placing the cool mayonnaise on the sunburn stopped the crying, as the vinegar in the mayonnaise cured the pain. To take the burn out of sunburn, use mayonnaise.

About going into debt (for any reason), wait seven days to see if the shine is still there. This little wait will save you lots of money and pain. Never lie, steal, cheat, or exaggerate. You will get caught. Set your goals for the future. What's the reason? What's the purpose? Write them down, because you can forget them.

Under all conditions, protect yourself. You are most important. If you are unable, you can help no one.

If you or any of your friends experience hot feet, massage the hot feet with wintergreen rubbing alcohol morning and night. The hot feet will go away in four or five days. It has worked for me and my stepdaughter, among others.

Legalizing weed, also known as pot, will create more users. In Colorado City, Colorado, it is legal. Recently, I was informed that on every street crossing in Colorado City there are four or five druggies begging for money to buy drugs. I do not know whether this is true. I do know that the person who told me this had just returned from Colorado City. I just read where unemployment is very low there. In fact, there are not enough people wanting a job to fill the need.

And I just saw on television today (July 2017) that they are running out of pot in Colorado. They can't grow enough to satisfy the users.

My life has been good. With this job, there were not too many dull moments. I really want to tell you how much I enjoyed writing this book. It makes me feel extra good that I have not lied or exaggerated one word. My eighty-five years have totaled awesome.

When I pass on, I hope I have a smile on my face.

Bye,

Banty Rooster

Epilogue

Six weeks ago I woke up at five o'clock in the morning with a very painful ache in my right arm and forearm. Being almost eighty-six years old, I understand about heart attacks and blocked arteries and their effect. The pain did not feel like a cramp or a charley horse. I had heard that violent coughing was first aid for heart attack or blocked arteries, so I began to cough as hard as I could, and the pain lessened.

When I stood up, I found that I was weak when it came to walking. Later I went to the emergency room at a medical center where they couldn't find anything wrong with my heart, blood pressure, blood sugar, and so forth. The doctor scheduled physical and pulmonary therapy, among other things. Not wanting to get wrapped up into having to be tied down to physical therapy for the next six months, I started walking on a treadmill and using a stationary bicycle. When I started, I could walk the treadmill for only three minutes and use the bicycle for three minutes. Now I am up to ten minutes on the treadmill and fifteen minutes on the stationary bicycle. This exercising completely remade my life. Yesterday I mowed my own lawn, which is a corner lot. All of this happened in five weeks and was worth every bit of it!

Made in the USA
Las Vegas, NV
12 April 2022

47334401R00066